Then to Zen

My Transformation

How I found my Glow and Let go

My small secrets to a healthier lifestyle

When, where, how? And what the hell am I doing?

I'm not entirely sure when it really started, but I think the defining moment that I realised, I fell out of love with myself was the breakdown of my long relationship with my young son's father, 11 years ago.

Never having been in a grown-up relationship where trust was a word that actually meant something, I suppose I wasn't that surprised when it ended. It was sad, it was painful, it was hard. But I came to the conclusion it was inevitable.

I got upset. I got angry. I wallowed in self-pity. I lurched from one disastrous relationship to another, attracting partners who only served to reinforce my belief that all relationships were toxic and, when they ended, that it's just how things went.

I realise now that I have always attracted distrust, and thrown myself into challenging relationships, because I simply didn't trust who I was, I didn't trust myself, my intuition or my heart.

I believed I didn't deserve to be loved. I just wasn't good at relationships. I wasn't one of those good people, like my friends and family around me, who deserved happiness and contentment with someone else.

That kind of loving relationship was as far-fetched a concept for me to imagine experiencing as walking on the moon. My norm was relationships that were hard and uncomfortable and not at all good for me.

There was help, of course. And I am so conscious now of the efforts made by my Mum and my friends, who tried so hard to support and encourage me to get help. And I tried it.

But it was help that I now know wasn't ok for me at that time, inwardly or outwardly. Because the real problem was that I did not love myself, my journey to this discovery wasn't an easy one.

Like a lot of people, I constantly sought
definition of who I am, how successful,
happy, confident, simply ok I could
be, by looking outside of myself. Being
defined by other people.

I suffered with self-doubt, self-criticism
and self-protection. It was like a
separation anxiety, finding it safer to not
let anyone get too close, just in case they
left and took part of me with them.

Funny really, I had already lost who I
was, how could they take anything from
me.

Things simply had to change.

There was only one relationship getting
in the way of me ever finding true
happiness. The relationship with myself.

And so, it began.

I needed something different, something new.

I found a new focus in fitness training. I passionately threw myself into the gym and I loved it. I thrived on the improvements I saw, and I had a sense of self-appreciation, buoyed by endorphins and body awareness. And I wanted to see how capable I was of progressing.

Finally, I started to see success in myself. And it was a nice feeling. I was good at something, something I could go on to share and help others.

I was driven and excited and I enthusiastically set off on a journey to create an approachable, friendly, informative and genuine business that helped others see that they, too, could succeed.

I wanted to show others
who, perhaps, lived with self-doubt or indecisiveness, they too could do this, that I believed in them and I would be with them every step of the way.

Women started to attend my
Bootcamps, fitness classes and one-to-one personal training sessions. And they thrived exactly as I
had, feeling more confident and comfortable, always thanking me for the support and influence. And that made me feel better and better.

I loved what I did, and for years it kept growing and gaining a reputation for excellent results.

I responded by giving more and more of myself to help everyone I could.

I would freely give out advice whenever asked. I relished the external approval, and placed no boundaries on my own worth or value as I constantly kept giving out to others, while there was no giving back to myself.

The impact finally started to take its toll. When people took what they could get and then left, it felt like a break-up. I took it as personal rejection, rather than focusing on the success I had helped them achieve, or that I had been instrumental in helping them move on and go further.

There were – and still are – many who stayed, who keep maintaining and improving, who enjoy the camaraderie of the atmosphere I have created, and who encourage others to share and enjoy.

But what comes with caring too much about everyone else, and excluding your

own needs and self-worth, while
you are giving too much to others?

I found myself increasingly re-focusing
more on the ones that dented my
armour, than on those who
were building me up. And, well, the
reality catches up with you. All the
thoughts, fears and doubts of the past re-
emerge and take over.

What comes with putting on your oxygen
mask last, after first helping everyone
else, as your plane comes
crashing down?

You run out of breath and, in turn, you
cannot help a soul.

You break.

That was very a significant and decisive
moment of realisation for me, because I
had faced that for real. I was a passenger

on that fateful plane in 1999 that crash-landed in Gerona, Spain, running off the end of the runway in a terrible storm, and breaking into pieces on the grass verge.

We were so fortunate to survive that. But such a profound experience doesn't leave you without scars, and it took a long time to learn to cope with the overwhelming sense of panic I suffered, on and off, in the years that followed.

It was the sense of not being able to control what was happening or how it made me feel, of trying to breathe and keep going, of fighting to help others around me, though all the time it was me that was breaking.

That was how I was starting to feel again.

So, after years focused on helping others, I thought what I needed was a new challenge to push me out of my comfort zone and pay some attention to me.

At least that's what I believed I was doing.

Instead, I had a client who wanted to train as a bodybuilder and I believed that, learning how to train her properly for that ambition would be good for me.

I brushed aside the nagging thought that this wasn't about paying attention to me at all, but about giving out to someone else. Familiar ground.

Instead, I worked with another personal trainer who said he could guide me on how to prepare people for bodybuilding competitions. And that guidance involved me doing it myself, learning through first hand experience. I felt and explained I should experience it for myself and I knew that, if I wanted to truly understand it, I needed to.

After all, isn't that what I do well, helping others to achieve their goals?

It started out with an agreement and plan that I would do enough to, just once, experience what it took to be on that stage, competing against the best.

I committed to the training programme, driven by wanting to help my client with her ambition. And, inevitably I guess, I eventually committed to a relationship with him.

It was a relationship increasingly founded on seeking his validation, massaging his ego and coping with his manipulation. And it was bound to fail, leaving me, once again, believing I simply wasn't good enough.

Determined not to fail in my quest, despite the end of the relationship, I set out to find a female coach, one I could trust.

This felt like safe ground and she ultimately helped me discover that, rather than training others to succeed on the stage, what I needed was to prove I could do it for myself. But prove to whom?

That's a question I wish I had asked myself at the time. But, I didn't.

Instead, I became absorbed in social media bullshit, stories about how this would advance my career, because only Personal Trainers with a rippling six pack and able to boast success on the stage could really claim the right to say they were any good.

And, well fast-forward a few months. I got the bug.

That first year of competing I gave my all. Everything revolved around it. I sacrificed time, meals and nights out, socialising, nice food and even good sleep. I sacrificed precious time with my son, friends and family.

But I loved it. The focus, the adrenaline, the attention, and the external recognition and approval that came with achieving success in this competitive world.

And succeed I did. I won competitions. I earned respect and recognition on a reputable & world recognised stage. I had media attention, photo-shoots and, yes, even some adulation from others who lived in that world.

In all honesty, I don't have too many regrets about that first year and the experience I had. I made new and dear friends, and the memory of sheer pleasure at eating a burger after months of deprivation is one I will always cherish.

So, I had done it. I had achieved what I set out to do. I entered three more competitions that year, doing well enough every time to feel I could justify and enjoy the "I'm good enough" label I had allowed myself, and I could go back to my life.

I was WRONG!!!

I managed to tuck away all the thoughts of sacrifices I had made, and instead I increasingly judged myself on why wasn't I better. I started putting on weight and soon became obsessed with my body image. My feelings of self-worth alternated with self-loathing. I cried, and I battled with my demons, because all I could see was that I was letting go of all that I had worked so hard for.

I started refusing to eat certain
foods, only to binge again when
I realised there was no pressure to
perform on stage any time soon, and I
would then eat them with abandon. I
simply couldn't handle "normal" anymore
.

I needed my focus and concentration
consumed so that I would not have to
face real life. I couldn't adjust and I
quickly resorted to wishing the days,
weeks and months away.

I turned back to the draw of competition
and all the validation that comes with it.
I counted down the months until,
trained to perfection, body toned and
tanned and mind focused, I was good
enough to stand proud.

I had more success, on the outside.
But internally my heart was breaking. I
knew I had convinced myself to do this to
feel good, but what I really felt was

shattered and hungry, and a little bit more broken.

Another competition done, another round of the self-doubt and I began torturing myself with questions "Where am I going?" "What am I doing?" "Why?" "What is my purpose?"

The questions were too uncomfortable to confront. So instead, I resorted to a spiral of 'rest.... and repeat'.

The success continued, but I was no longer competing for proof of anything. I was running away from who I really was when I wasn't that person on stage. I was simply running away from being ME.

I couldn't believe I was good enough without the trophy, the false attention from men, the words of admiration and even the misplaced belief that this was right for me'. Maybe I simply didn't want to.

I told myself that I had a plan, I was always forward thinking, always getting up for a goal.

I threw myself further into this world. But rather than living my life, I started simply existing in this one. I was strong and outwardly bold, with a hugely determined hard energy. I was focused, and I successfully blocked out anything that existed beyond this existence.

My soft side did not get a look in. My empathy decreased. I dismissed emotional engagement, believing being sensitive would hurt me.

I told myself I was happy. I lied to myself every day. I still hurt, but I ignored the pain and nagging doubt.

In reality, I was simply avoiding my true self. I craved and thrived on external validation.

Then I met someone who I thought was different. He was from my 'new world' of bodybuilding and I allowed myself to believe I was happy. Although I know friends and family close to me were increasingly worried about my lifestyle, we seemed to go well together and people liked him.

My son enjoyed having him around and, together, we were all blissfully happy. At least for a while. Until, that is, it all fell apart

The last time I stood on stage, he proposed to me.

He surprised me, down on one knee, and presenting me with the most beautiful ring, It was perfect, the ring that I had told him I always wanted, but I never really expected to get.

My ego wanted it so much, needed it even. The diamond, the love story, the romance, the happy ever after.

But, in truth, my heart knew I wanted a different life from him.

We had met through my journey of self-neglect and emotional dismissal.

It was not the real me. It was the lure of the stage, his validation and his pleasure in my success.

He wanted all of the stage, the attention the approval I had come to realise was not real.

Although I didn't allow myself to think it then, it was destined for failure.

Our break-up was a shock to my system, harsh and painful and embarrassing. Another relationship had ended, and I quickly realised that my competitor lifestyle was ending too.

I went through a really bad patch then, and I know everyone was worried about me. I could see their concern, but I couldn't do anything about it.

What would people think... how would I move on...what next...where do I go from here?"

What the HELL am I doing?

My breakdown was not pretty.

I did not want to wake up.

My beautiful, thoughtful, sensitive son looked on fearfully as his mother fell apart, knowing but not

understanding in his child
innocence, why I was so unhappy?

He did not like that I
continued competing after having to
compete for my love and attention. He
was treading on eggshells, and his
concern and care for me contrasting his
young years. It was like he could see
through me when no one else could.

Enough.......

Eventually, I threw myself back into my
work as a personal trainer. If I
was helping other people achieve their
goals, I'd feel better, I'd be better for it.

It worked for a short while, but deep
down I recognised it wasn't the
answer. And then, I suddenly I knew for
certainty that what I really needed was to
do some serious work on myself. For
myself.

It was the beginning... but it was no walk in the park.

I ate the fruit again. And I cried

I started focusing on what used to make me feel good, being healthy, being a good mum and helping others.

But this time, I included myself.

I ate fresh fruit and started to create and develop classes for everyone who might want to join me.

I stepped away from the heavy weights and re-introduced my body back to the real picture of how I wanted to be.

I cried a little less every day.

And I fell back
in love with progress, seeing
improvement moving and thriving again
in a healthy, happy way.

I focused on good nutrition, my son and I
cooking and creating meals together.

I started Yoga, Meditation and healthy
exercise.

My classes with my clients felt so
rewarding again. They were enjoying
their sense of achievement and
progress, and I was relishing their
enjoyment.

I was returning to my roots, the stuff that
got me on this path in the first place, my
why, my purpose, my reason.

Instead of seeking external validation,
I started looking inward, learning to
respect and love myself.

I began questioning why I felt I was so undeserving of my own love, of giving myself time and care, rather than believing it was others who deserved it more.

Why did I not see I was deserving of the same attention that I gave to others?

Why did I treat myself like an unwanted friend, cruel and bullying and filled only with disdain for who I am?

I did not love who I was, because I believed I had to be more, better, different. Maybe if I 'became' something else, I'd be good enough to earn love and respect.

Was this true?

Of course not. Not at all.

I realised then, that I deserved my time, my care, my love and my friendship.

This time I was going to give it.....to myself.

An awakening

I was going to do things very differently this time, and even the concept of this new approach filled me with optimistic anticipation.

It started with discovering the true power and meaning of Meditation.

So what is it, exactly? Well many, I know, think it is wishy-washy, all candles and spiritual mind, body and soul, and it is an uncomfortable notion for a lot of people.

But break through the preconceptions, and you quickly discover that

Meditation is all about who and what you are, what you need to love and live with yourself successfully.

Let's start with your physical needs and wellbeing.

The body needs fuel, care, flexibility, activity and nurturing to work properly. Just like brushing our teeth or taking a bath, or walking the dogs, our body needs time, effort and input to be part of our daily routine!

Translated, that means no more output – giving to others -
 without embracing input – doing it for

yourself, caring for, protecting and nurturing for your own sake.

While many of us find it easier to focus on physical health and fitness, going to the gym, running and achieving physical goals, the mind is an altogether harder tool to power up, learn to control and put to good use.

It is an incredibly powerful tool. It can make us believe, it can bring us down, it can build confidence and just as easily destroy it. If we don't learn how to use and control our minds constructively, it is prone to overthinking, with negative thoughts breeding negative feelings.

However, with the right mindfulness tool, your mind can be an incredibly powerful ally, a very beautiful thing, as one with your body.

The soul - the being, the heart, the life, the energy, the very core to all you are, beliefs, feelings and presence.

All of YOU as YOU are.

Do not ignore your soul, in order to conform

To ignore your soul is to never live your own life.

Letting Go and Finding Harmony

So how did meditation bring all these together for me?

I started by simply giving myself the time to find, appreciate and enjoy energy, quiet, and caring.

I started to think 'well' of myself, not just others. I learned to appreciate the present moment, my health, my life, my heart, my true being.

The difference was tangible and genuine. My son started to notice and I was suddenly conscious of the calming and happy effect that my changes were having on his wellbeing and confidence. Even my dog, Champ, sensed the change, as the quiet, the calm and the self-caring started to fill my home.

It was mirrored around me, it was palpable, and I had not done anything extreme except to find my way to becoming well again.

I gave up coffee and cut down on refined sugars as much as I could, a major challenge for me, but one that I quickly adapted to as I discovered mindfulness eating.

I started to smile. A lot! Something I hadn't really done much of lately. Just waking up and taking a deep
breath, looking forward to moving my body for 20-30 mins before meditation, brought a sense of joy and calm.

My day was neither a 'good day' nor a 'bad day', it just was. I learned to stop labelling everything as successful
or otherwise by the level of 'good' I placed on.

Not always feeling good was ok. And if I had not managed to do something, that was ok too.

I prioritised my health, my time and my family. And it was paying off.

I didn't really focus on what others might be thinking of
this profound transformation, and hadn't really paid any attention to whether I considered it mattered to me or not.

But suddenly the comments became very obvious. Friends, family and clients complimented me on how well I was looking. I became aware that my skin, hair, nails, body, eyes and inner-glow showed. I was feeling good and I was more content than I can remember being for a very long time. I didn't feel the need for external validation, but I won't pretend I wasn't delighted that suddenly people noticed.

What was really going on?

The binge eating and the restrictive eating patterns I had become addicted to as a way of coping had subsided. I no longer resorted to overeating and neglecting my inner thoughts in the constant battle to defeat self-doubt, and chronic lack of self-worth.

I had stopped consuming the lies I told myself.

I finally cracked it. I was worthy. I was good enough. I did care about myself. It was ok to love myself, wholly and without contempt.

I slept, really slept well for the first time in a long time. My night-time habits had gone from going to bed anxious and agitated, facing constant broken sleep, and often getting up and pacing around several times a night, to winding down with a herbal tea in the fresh air, before retiring to bed with a book, putting the phone down after setting it to do not disturb, and enjoying the time to relax and gently drift off to sleep.

The lack of caffeine obviously helped with my sleeping patterns, but also my mind had stopped racing, constantly beating itself-up. I bought a weighted blanket. Wow, now that is like getting a big, comforting, gentle hug in bed. I also use a lovely natural organic magnesium butter for my feet which I recommend further on.

Getting a good night's sleep is essential
to wellbeing and health is no secret.
Yet so many of us underestimate the vital
part it plays in the wellness
of body, mind and soul.

Sleep is life's natural tonic, and
a good eight hours of rest can change a
person.

I journaled how I felt daily, and
whenever else I needed to, I would sit
and write about how I was feeling,
refusing to bottle everything up inside.

I stopped judging myself for how I was
feeling and criticising my emotions. I
reminded myself that none of it was
permanent and no blame had to be
attached to past or present thoughts. It
just was.

I let go of perfection.

I learned to accept that to get
somewhere in life, I didn't always have to
be in control of everything. I didn't have
to dictate how my days would go,
planning
everything in detail, marking out a 'to
do' list like a teacher looking for an A*

I binned the list and started to
trust myself and my judgement.

If I had to prioritise, I would write one
thing that I needed to, and I
wouldn't move on until that was
done. What I was doing in that
moment was what mattered, not
thinking, planning or worrying
about what was next.

I ditched the strict diets
and eating plans.

I made a promise to aim for colourful, flavoursome and, wherever possible, for natural.

Instead of a restrictive diet, I could choose what I wanted with these three intentions.

I found myself munching on fruit or carrots, making cucumber water and adding fresh ginger, lime and lemon to my food. I started making little tapas meals as a way of trying different things. And my son joined me. He learned to love baking and cooking, and got as excited about trying out new, healthy meals as I was.

I ordered fresh vegetables and fruit to be delivered weekly, leaving it to my local supplier to determine what I have, and then get excited about being creative with what arrives, filling the slow cooker with all colours, and aiming for super healthy combinations.

We started eating more mindfully,
phones down and engaging in
conversation about the food and
taste. My son and I, discussing what
we were cooking and eating,
and enjoying spending that time together
in the moment, all the
while, encouraging us both to be open to
trying new things.

So, my advice, ditch focusing on the "I
can't have" and turn it into "I choose..."

I discarded the mobile phone and social
media expectations,
acknowledging the reality that a
filtered version of what everyone else
was doing, or crazy numbers of
followers, would do neither me nor my
business any good!

I wanted a real, genuine connection with
people, and to work with them in
achieving results that benefited both
sides. I recognised that helping 10 real
people to genuinely achieve real results

meant far more
than attracting 10,000 virtual followers,
simply to fulfil a social media
dictate of expectations in defining
success.

My health, frame of mind and, more
importantly, the time and sense of
genuine satisfaction became far more
rewarding to me than more 'likes'.

The truth is, real people will see the
genuine in you, will value your glow, and
will be inspired to want that glow of
achievement and self- esteem too.

I learned all this, and consciously
decided to put all my energy, enthusiasm
and passion into promoting, encouraging
and supporting Mindful, Healthy, Fit
and Happy living.

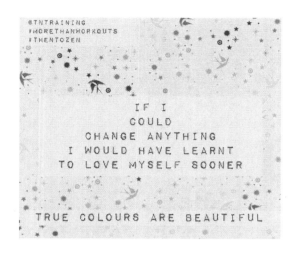

@TNTRAINING
#MORETHANWORKOUTS
#THENTOZEN

IF I
COULD
CHANGE ANYTHING
I WOULD HAVE LEARNT
TO LOVE MYSELF SOONER

TRUE COLOURS ARE BEAUTIFUL

Loving the Flow... Embracing the Glow

My real life now is so far removed from the destructive and disenchanted focus of recent years, that it is hard to imagine how I got here.

But the flow of my life now is so calm, gentle, fulfilling and rewarding, that I cannot help but want to share the immensely engaging sense of wellbeing with others, to inspire and encourage you to embrace the glow that comes with learning to love yourself.

I am kind to myself now. I like who I am, and I like how that makes me with other people. I am better for it

I spoil myself.

I run the biggest bubbliest baths, and I relax and enjoy every bubbly moment of it.

I set aside 30 mins every morning, just for me.

I allow time before bed, to sit outside and take in the fresh air.

I choose to read books that inspire my healthy way of living and mindfulness.

I light my favourite candles, even if it is just for me.

I started painting and decorating my home, the way I want it, rather than how others tell me I should do it.

I landscaped my garden, and I mean I did it, learning new gardening skills and joyfully creating a haven that I now get to relish either in my own headspace, with my son, or with friends and family. I relax listening to the water feature, meditating and feeding the beautiful birds that visit my birdhouse daily.

I walk the dogs with my son, and do not think I could be or should be doing something else, just simply enjoying the time, the experience and his company.

I cook us beautiful, tasty, healthy meals.

I take trips to the beach, just to take in the view and watch the waves.

I exercise daily with my 'tntraining' clients, and how I enjoy the lift I get from their efforts and enthusiasm to succeed with the workouts

I cuddle up with the dogs at my feet, the fire on and the tv off, just listening to my favourite music and relishing the chance for quiet contemplation.

I meditate and appreciate my life.

I set goals for myself; ones that will make me happy, not aiming for goals that will satisfy, impress or earn validation from other people

I journal my thoughts, and take my time to understand my feelings

I spend quality, fun time with my son, without one eye on the clock, or checking my phone. I make our time OUR time and, let him know how important he is to me.

Recycling

When I started to realise I did not lack
anything, that I had so much I didn't
need, spending money on things just
to try to make myself feel better, I started
recycling and giving more to charity.

I saved money. I stopped trying to look
for that next purchase to make me feel
good. I started caring more about what I
should do to feel better for myself. I
focused on being healthy internally and
adapting my daily habits to those that
were better for all the right reasons.

Now I enjoy separating the recycling and
sorting through my things so I can fill
bags for charity. The sense of doing
something to help someone else, with no
expectation of anything in return, is so
simple, it is reward itself.

So why hold onto something just in case,
for that possible special occasion, that

"I'll maybe wear it or use it one day",
when someone else could be making use
of that today.

Live now and live well. It is a simple
message.

It is about self-care. But truly caring for
yourself brings with it a desire to help
and care for others however you can.

It is such a beautiful way of being.

We are all in this together, we all live on
this earth together, yet we see
it divided by so much
hatred, prejudice, greed, false validation,
selfishness and ignorance.

To be able to love and want to help
others, you need to first love and help
yourself. Everything flows from that.
And when you do, you and everyone you
touch throughout your life, those you
know and those you don't, will benefit
from it.

What a powerful message that is.

Equilibrium is the key

To achieve such balance in your life, you need to care for your body, your mind and your soul.

But you don't have to fix everything all at once. It is a journey, a process that you can achieve in your own time and in your own way. My advice is to focus on finding one thing to improve on, and work on it until it becomes a healthy habit. In turn, that will invite more healthy habits and good intentions to follow.

Appreciate the day from the start

I wake up every morning, pull the curtains back and, whatever the weather, I say 'thank you' three times…

Thank you for life, as it is, and I smile a great big smile.

Smiling causes a physiological change in the body and brings so many benefits.

Here's an experiment. Stand with your hands on your hips, think about something that makes you feel sad, and then, keeping your hips facing forward, try turning your upper body to look behind you. Do that on both sides.

Then, face front and take a few moments to think of something happy, something that genuinely makes you smile, and repeat the exercise. I can almost guarantee you will be able to turn further and see more behind you than you did the first time.

Give it a try! It is inspiring.

Smiling can bring a joy of its own, and it can also make you feel excited about what's ahead. Just be happy to be awake, with a new day ahead of you, full of potential and promise and experiences that, one way or another, will help shape your life.

It can set you up for the day and bring you a sense of gratitude for all that you have.

Water is the elixir of life

I stay hydrated.

We are water!!!

The average human body is made up of
57-70% water. We need it for everything
to work properly. There is
no simpler way to put it, if you don't keep
it topped up, your body will fail you. It
is like driving your car without any fuel
to feed the engine and expecting it not to
break down!

Dehydration is serious business. At best,
it causes headaches, poor digestion and
fatigue. At worst, it can lead to
organ damage and other serious
conditions. The message is clear. Stay
hydrated, stay well, stay healthy.

I gave up alcohol.

Now, I'm not preaching and I'm not pretending that I don't enjoy a glass of wine or two on the occasional social event.

But I used to look to alcohol to help me deal with life, to face my fears, escape my disappointments, and, well, just to get out of my own space

Alcohol, certainly when exceeding moderation, lowers our inhibitions, masks self-doubt, blinds us to our better judgement and avoids us having to deal with reality.

But the reality is still there when you have only the hangover and toxins to help you face up to it, to highlight the very things you are trying to escape.

My new focus on life means I no longer need it. When I want to wind down, to manage a challenging situation, to face up to disappointment or confront my fears, I no longer feel the need to turn to alcohol as my first resort.

Instead, I turn to myself and focus on what matters. A balance of body, mind and soul will be a far greater friend in sorting things out in the long run. And not a hangover in sight!

Au naturel

Skincare, hair, teeth... small changes can make a huge difference.

I no longer feel the need to use heavy coverage foundations, because my skin is being looked after with good food, water, good sleep and regular exercise.

I use light natural moisturisers, touch up any blemishes and apply a little highlighter, all of them as natural as possible.

I swapped heavy toothpastes in favour of natural versions, with coconut as a main ingredient, and my teeth are the whitest I've ever known them.
Obviously, my cutting down on coffee helped too, though I
still enjoy the occasional decaffeinated when the mood takes me.

I opted for all-natural face wash, and for my bath, add rock salts and essential oils.

More mindful of my shopping habits, I found I was becoming equally mindful of how my purchases were impacting the environment, while my wallet is taking much less of a hit too.

I was always easily influenced by the clever marketing around expensive products being better, but I wish I'd discovered years ago , the real value of natural products, the more natural the healthier for the body, mind, soul and, often, the pocket.

I'm not sponsored by any products, so I feel comfortable including here a list of natural products I have found that have worked for me and may be useful.

Teeth – Biomed super white 99% natural

Hair – Tropical Isle – Jamaican black castor oil

Hair – Evolve daily apple hair and body wash

Face- Evolve Organic Beauty daily detox facial wash and cleansing melt

Face – Evolve Climate Veil Tinted Light

Face – Evolve Gold facemask is luxury

Face – The Ordinary every product so far

Sleep – Sweet Bee organics magnesium butter

Skin – Sweet Bee – Sacred Skin bundle

Hair & Skin – organic coconut oil

Bath – Epsom Salts / Chunks of Salt

Face mask – Farryn Amber skincare – Rose facial mask

Face – Luna goddess night serum

Body – Sintra – Naked Body Butter

Love the Skin you're in

I started Dry Body Brushing, it seemed too simple to make that much difference, but I noticed an immediate effect on my skin. The process itself is uplifting and it leaves you with the softest skin.

I highly recommend it and doing it mindfully, grateful for the body you have and appreciating every part of you.

This small body care routine is a genuine a treat and has changed my mind-set on how I look at my shape and my skin. Although I constantly pushed myself in fitness training, too often I neglected the after care, paying too little attention to the small details that I thought were unimportant.

I am happy to stand corrected. The small details are vital. Like a precious painting, a little attention to detail and treating it with respect, care and love can transform a picture into a work of art that you can appreciate and enjoy looking at every day.

I would highly recommend a good body brush and body cream to follow as an excellent investment.

Face-off

<u>I started going out without my make up on.</u>

I was, I confess, something of a makeover addict, changing my whole appearance every few weeks, hair colour, make-up, style. I loved every minute of the experience, and with a hairdresser for a best friend, it was easy to be adventurous, finding creative new ways to hide my insecurities and feel safe behind another bold new look.

It was a deeper need than anyone, including me, realised, as I increasingly invested my self-confidence in a programme of change. In truth, I couldn't ever accept I was "good enough" just being me, so I hid behind a costume and mask.

Unveil bold new look; enjoy initial sense of misplaced confidence; regress to self-loathing; Repeat.

I was obsessed with keeping my makeup mask on, touching it up every hour even between work- out sessions.

I never allowed my skin to breathe and, breaking out in workout sweats with a face covered in makeup, was a recipe for disaster in my skin care. I'd just use more make-up to cover the consequences.

So I removed it all and watched startled as my skin quickly improved. It was such a rewarding feeling that I refused to cake my skin again. Of course, everyone loves to feel special sometimes, especially when going out, and I wanted to find a way I could embrace my natural with a touch of date night out if ever needed.

I embraced natural skin-care and make-up products, and I have never looked back.

Hair-raising days pay off

Next, my hair needed the same touch of kindness, and I started working with my dear hairdresser friend to bring it back to its natural health and let it grow naturally. Having had extensions for many years, it's a big ask, and I've had to accept a long period of stripped-back hair-up days.

But I remind myself that the bigger picture is worth it and I smile now, because treating my hair with love and care supports me in being my true self. I actually find myself getting emotional when I leave the hairdressers these days, embracing my own self.

I no longer hide my softer style,
and every time I leave the
hairdresser it seems different. It
is growing longer, healthier and better
and it is all mine!

It hasn't been an easy one,
but totally worth it.

Vitamins for life

The benefits of taking vitamins have been
long advanced and, although there are
different views, there is general
acknowledgement that the right vitamins
in the right way are good for health and
well-being.

5 Benefits of Taking Multivitamins Daily

Increased energy levels

When you don't get enough vitamins, your body has to work harder to perform simple tasks, which can lead to fatigue and other health problems

Improved mood

Reduces stress and anxiety

Improved short-term memory

Maintained muscle strength

Vitamin C, also known as ascorbic acid, has several important functions. helping to protect cells and keeping them healthy. maintaining healthy skin, blood vessels, bones and cartilage and helping with wound healing.

Multi Vitamins are valued particularly where some people find it tricky to get all the vitamins and minerals they need through a balanced diet. The body needs 13 vitamins to maintain health and wellbeing, and many of them contain nutrients, which the body cannot reproduce itself, so we have to get them from our food.

Vitamin D - contributes to the maintenance of normal bones and normal functioning of the immune system. I always think of it as the sunshine vitamin.

In a perfect world, we'd all be able to get what we need to replenish our body stocks through healthy eating, but that's not always possible, and supplements can play a major role in helping.

There are many vitamin and mineral brands on the market.

I like Solgar Skin, nail and hair formula, in particular, which contains a blend of vitamins specifically for hair, skin and nails an excellent addition to my healthy diet, with results that speak for themselves.

Aiding and abetting healthy nutrition

Herbal medicines and remedies have been around for thousands of years and I have discovered a number that have been instrumental in helping me on my path to better, healthier, happier and more content living.

Of course, everyone is different, and you should always check with your GP if you are taking any medications or have identified health issues or conditions, before taking supplements.

I am not sponsored by any product manufacturer or supplier, and I am happy to share with you some information on the ones that have worked for me personally.

I have always suffered with premenstrual symptoms and *'Natures aid PremEeze'* *is* a traditional herbal medicinal product used to help relieve such as irritability; mood swings; breast tenderness; bloating and menstrual cramps. These have helped me massively.

Ashwagandha has been used in Ayurvedic medicine for thousands of years. Commonly thought of as the Indian Ginseng, this amazing herb has been shown to reduce stress in difficult times and increase stamina when you need it most. It has worked for me.

Organic Super Greens powder is great for energy, immune function, mental performance, antioxidant and weight management. I usually use it to make a fresh cucumber, lime, lemon and ginger water to add my greens and take my supplements.

Herbal teas are perfect from waking up to going to bed. I particularly love the loose teas and, now a favourite, the Spiral Tea bundle, which is delicious, refreshing & calming.

I emphasise that these are my personal preferences for supplements that have helped me. I am not advocating any of them as 'miracle treatments or cures', they are just part of my daily life and I have felt the benefits.

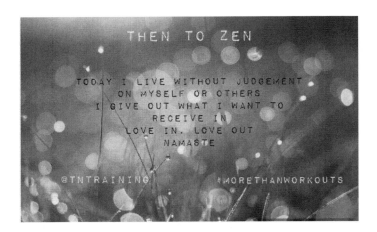

Turn up the music up to dance... and even do the chores

I have never been a fan of cleaning and housework,

I would always rather be in the gym, doing what I love. But chores have to be done and a nice home does make you feel good.

Have you ever found a way to make doing
a chore you don't like more fun, just to
get it done? Well, I've found my way of
mindfully make facing the chores more
enjoyable.

Instead of setting in stone certain days or
times to do chores, I just wait for a free
hour and then, with cloth in hand,
I BLAST the tunes and dive right in,
saying out loud, this is going to be FUN!

Washing the dishes, mopping the floors,
changing the beds or doing laundry, I
turn up the volume and sing along,
dancing through the chores with a
passion and new-found enthusiasm and
energy.

It's a great little workout, it really is fun
and, when I'm done, I take simple
pleasure in my nice clean home. I light a
beautiful smelling candle, sit down to
enjoy my work with my feet
up, and then run a huge salted bubbly
bath, filled with essential oils, to soak my

body, with the added bonus of making the whole house smell incredible.

A study in Moonlight

I have learned to really appreciate the world around me, and have developed a special love for the sun, the stars and the moon.

They are so very beautiful, filled with energy and light, and not much beats the pleasure of seeing a full moon. I get genuinely excited to see it every time.

If you don't believe me when I talk of the way it can lift your spirits, take a seat outside for the next full moon, and just look at it. I mean really look. Study its colour, the spherical shape, the shadows. It is an incredible golden orb of breath-taking beauty and you don't have to be spiritual, a hippy or a dreamer to take pleasure in such beauty surrounding us.

Be in the moment. Slow down enough to really SEE! Appreciate life! It is an unrivalled tonic for the soul.

A story of patience

I have always much struggled with reading, not to read words but having the patience to really read properly. I would mindlessly read a line, put it down, come back to it later and read that line again. And I'd probably not take a word of it in.

Finding meditation, putting my phone down, avoiding distractions and allowing myself time for me changed all that. Now I love reading. I absorb every line, engage with the content in every page and enjoy the story and its meaning.

There's few better ways to relax and enjoy life than reading, and now I find myself commending it wholly to anyone who will listen!

So, in that vein, I have listed a few of the books that I love and have inspired me to make this journey and flourish in the process.

Love and let go. - Rachel Brathen

On Being Human – Jennifer Pastiloff

Peace is every step-Thich Nhat Hanh

Simply Beautiful books.

Interesting choices

What things do you enjoy? What sparks your curiosity and feeds your soul?

Do you enjoy learning? To discover? To write? To paint? To get outdoors.

Is there something you used to love doing that you don't make time for anymore?

I've always loved being creative and inspired by things around me, and focusing on things that could help me or others has been a real joy.

I am also impulsive and ever so slightly impatient, so I do have to force myself to slow down sometimes, and accept that things, especially change, takes time. I've learned not to rush the process, but to enjoy the journey.

Take the Day Off

Sounds obvious, I know, but how many of us actually take days off. I mean really take the day. Not using it to rush around shopping, doing chores, catching up with emails, taking the children out, visiting family and so on.... but devoting the occasional day just to ourselves?

I used to fill my days off with endless chores, food shops, cleaning and days out. I wasn't going to waste that free time.

But oh gosh, how I was wasting that free time.

The day off, gone in a whirlwind of activity, and it was back to work again.

Now I take my day off, OFF! And I view these days as little magic pills of clarity, quiet and peace.

If I feel the urge to put something away or clean a little, it's because, it's in the moment, and that's what I choose to do.

If I meditate, watch a movie or cook a healthy meal, it's because that is what I choose to do.

I have stopped planning my day off like a to do list.

Of course, making plans in advance, perhaps to meet friends or do something special is different, providing that's what you want to do, and not because you feel you should.

And even then, if I suddenly didn't feel up to it on the day, I was longer afraid to say "Sorry, but it's really not a good for me today."

All this within reason, of course, because feeling like you are letting people down is stressful in itself. But it is ok to ask yourself how important it is to you, and to others who matter to you, and whether the consequences of going along with the plan will be more damaging to you than if you changed your mind.

Most of the time, making plans with friends is something to look forward to and can be the best part of your time off.

But when it is not, be honest with them. Really good friends will understand and support you. There'll be times when it is you on the other end of that, and you will need to be as understanding and supportive too.

Remember, rarely does anyone judge you more harshly than you judge yourself.

Let the inner child out and spend time with your family

Was there something you loved to do when you were young?

Did you enjoy certain movies?

Do you have memories you would love to recreate with your own children or young family members?

Who doesn't enjoy a day of Disney movies or colouring books?

Childlike innocence it's so good for the soul. As adults, we often lose sight of simple joy, we tend to take everything and everyday too seriously, and that's how you lose the magic.

So, let your inner child out, enjoy the simple things and the people around and view everything with content ment, love and joy. Just see and accept things for what they are.

A huge difference in my life has been learning to fully appreciate my family. They have supported me and been there for me through all phases, stages and challenges in my life, through good and bad, and they have never let me down.

I confess it has taken me a while to recognise that rather than thinking I had no time to spend with people that mattered because I was too busy trying to make something of my life, truth is, life is already beautiful when you take time to spend and share it with those you love.

Do everything and appreciate
everything, knowing everything will pass

Good : bad : dull : quiet : exciting : luck :
love : moments : seconds: hours : days:
years

Everything ends

So, if something makes you smile,

don't rush it

If something makes you sad, accept it

If something excites you, embrace it

If something scares you, breathe through
it

If something loves you, cherish it

If something hates you, let it go

If something makes you bounce out of
bed, appreciate it

If something challenges you, learn from
it

Nothing is forever, so be in this exact
moment, don't waste
the precious present
moment wondering what's next.

If something is not as you wish,
be reassured that it's not forever, it's just
right now.

Trust yourself enough to know that,
whatever happens, you can handle it.

Life is not against you, 'shit happens'! It
is how we respond that matters

"This too shall pass"

Your happiness is you, it is your
responsibility

Enjoy the journey

It probably goes without saying that all the things I talk about in my story have happened over time, it hasn't been an all-at-once epiphany that has changed my life overnight. But it has all made a massive difference and every change has been more than worth the effort.

I started with a meditation course.

I had started meditating and it was incredible, being scattered, busy and nonstop and always exhausting myself to be better. I could genuinely never have imagined having the time or the ability to still my ever so busy monkey brain.

That's when I realised, I needed this more than anything.

Once I had done this for myself, I was ready to learn more and able to help others.

This inspired me to undertake
a mindfulness and a yoga diploma,
through which I was able to combine
all my workout routines and my daily
life together with the need nurture and
nourish body, mind and soul.

It was a whole package, and I didn't have
to neglect anything or anyone. The whole
experience was breathtakingly inspiring.

Succeeding in that ambition, achieving a
Certificate of Distinction, was one of the
most rewarding things I've ever achieved,
and I won't pretend I wasn't proud as
punch. The congratulations from family
and friends only served to support my
belief that I was on the right path to a
balanced, healthier and happier life.

I am now practicing Buddhism and
meditation with a local Buddhist church,
and it is truly fascinating. I don't
generally find it easy to congratulate
myself, but I do feel truly proud of my

transformation and that I'm giving myself this time for myself.

Then to Zen

I Podcast. I know this is not for everyone. Like keeping a journal, some people find it relaxing and helpful and inspiring, while others just don't take to it at all, seeing it as a chore, which it should never be.

But, for me, stepping into the arena and opening up has provided me with another form of letting go. It is not about having to be perfect at it, but speaking my truth for myself, which in turn has helped others, And I know from feedback I get, that it is doing just that.

My message here is simple, open your heart, be true to yourself. That is what matters. It is not to win validation or seek agreement from others, but about being completely honest to yourself and to others, and if just one other person is encouraged by your honesty to do the same, that is a wonderful bonus.

Doing good things for your own wellbeing will, ultimately, help others around you too. *Fill your cup not first, but as well.*

Fit for Life- the Bedrock of my Goals

I couldn't write my story without turning to one of the most significant things in my life, the bedrock of my success and the foundation for changing my life for the better over the past few years.

I established TNTraining in 2010 based on a combined passion for keeping fit and being able to help others feel good about themselves.

A combination of one-to-one personal training, fitness classes, 'boot camp' sessions and personalised programmes has seen my business and professional reputation grow significantly, and it has given me the strength, incentive and opportunity to get to where I am today in my total transformation.

I work out with women who want the same thing, to look good and feel well; to give themselves the time and energy to enjoy life; to bounce out of bed in the morning feeling happy and healthy and energised, loving the body they're in; walking around and feeling great, naked and dressed in clothes, fit enough to keep up with life, family, pets & whatever else comes their way.

And I love it.

I can't begin to describe the sense of joy seeing them transforming from discontented, self-critical women, lacking self-esteem, to happy, healthy, pathfinders, self-assured, glowing and empowered to enjoy who they are and what they have and can continue to achieve.

My classes are created to encourage and support women from all walks of life, all ages and all levels of fitness, whether looking to tone up, lose body fat, improve health or just feel better about themselves, I've had the pleasure of watching them all reach and often exceed their goals and expectations.

We all know that the most challenging part of any workout programme is getting started and then keeping it up, maintaining motivation to turn up for classes or sessions when it is really the last thing you feel like. But just turning up is a win, and I make it my mission to keep them motivated to do so.

I've often said that if I could bottle up the feeling after every session is done, and then get them to sip it daily, they would never not turn up again.

Of course, life gets in the way. We all find it hard to fit everything into our days and, at times, exercise doesn't seem a priority. It's an easy 'put it off until tomorrow' target. But on those days you need someone to keep you going, and that's why we are all in this together.

I've said several times in my story already that it is all about small steps, making progress, being prepared to change, and lifestyle choices that will make a lifetime of difference. No fads, gimmicks or unrealistic diet plans, it is all about Real Women, Real Results.

This isn't a sales pitch for my business, but my way of acknowledging the role this mission and passion have had in my transformation and how important it has been to me to be able to use that to help others achieve their peace, harmony, happiness and balance.

Labelled..... Not this Pigeon

I've always resented stereotyping and
refuse to see what I do, and what
I believe in, simply pigeon-holed into a
PT label.

Yes, I do personal training. Yes, I help
people lose weight, shape up, get fitter,
healthier and happier. But everything I
have ever done has come from my heart.

Everyone is different. No two people are
exactly the same. And I don't believe in
pigeon-holing my clients or their
individual needs any more than I am
prepared to accept being pigeon-holed
myself.

So, Personal Trainer, Health Coach, Life
Coach, Motivator, Mentor, Creator,
Supporter, Trainer, Teacher, all helpful,
perhaps, descriptive titles, but labelling
is not for me.

If a client, a friend, a family member needed something I could help them with, I would do whatever it took to work with them and help them succeed.

What I don't know, I will seek out and learn. I am interested more in adapting to meet their needs, than I am in them being shoehorned into a set of exercise rules and existing classes.

It is fair to say that there was a time when I found myself trying to fit the label I was being given, but it led only to me losing sight of their individual needs and my own beliefs and standards. It was the time I increasingly abandoned my own oxygen mask while too busy trying help others with theirs, not recognising that I was really helping neither of as well as I could.

That has all changed now and I am confident my clients and my professional and personal reputation are better served for it.

I choose no one single label. I am! I do! I help. It is as simple as that.

LESSONS I HAVE LEARNED ALONG THE WAY

Perfection is not perfect

Perfection, the very word used to make me want more and to be more. It led me to constantly analyse and critique my very being every day.

I would look at things about me and judge them to be imperfect and be left with a sense of overwhelming failure, a belief that I lacked all the skills and talents and knowledge that I needed to succeed.

It made me anxious about the future. How could I possibly be perfect?

We all do this to ourselves to some degree. We beat ourselves up, we do not treat ourselves with compassion, understanding and kindness.

But the point is, who is to say it was not perfect? Who decides that I lacked these things in my life? What court would I be attending to accuse and determine me as an imperfect person or a failure for achieving perfection?

I used to believe being hard on myself, made me achieve my goals, stopped me giving in and I often wonder how different our experiences would be if we believed in ourselves, if we accepted we are good enough for the things we do and have in life.

I imagine it would have brought many goals to fruition a lot quicker and the journey would have been pleasurable.

Thankfully, I've learned that it is not about be perfect or the being best of everyone. It is about trying to be the best version of me, achieving the best I can be. And for that, I feel fully qualified, thank you.

As I go forward with this piece of information it's amazing how much more I give back to myself with encouragement and positivity, I enjoy a lot more of what I achieve, and not just at the end of the race, but every single step towards the finishing line.

Reaching out for help

One very valuable lesson I have learned through my transformation, is that reaching out to others is not a weakness, it is not failing, it is not saying you cannot cope alone.

Everyone needs someone at some time. It may be a friend, a partner, family member, a professional expert, a mentor. And there will be times when others will reach out to you for help.

You would not judge them as a failure for doing that...so why judge it in yourself.

Respond instead of Reacting

Like many people, I believed that to assert myself and stand my ground, I had to defend. I had to be reactive, be strong, be firm and not give in. I don't dismiss that reaction as always the wrong thing to do, but I do realise now, with the wisdom of self-discovery and hindsight, that my way of dealing with challenging situations created drama in my life and, sometimes, pain for others.

I have, through benefit of studying Buddhism, come to realise that to react instead of respond is to not hear, feel or see things as they truly are to yourself or others.

I now choose to take space for myself before responding and 9 out of 10 times my response is a lot better than how I originally would have reacted.

You know that there are some things you can control and influence, and equally things that you cannot.

Learn to recognise the difference, to have the confidence to question your thinking and reactions, to ask yourself whether there could be another version to your thinking when self-doubt appears.

If I find myself facing a stressful situation or difficult scenario, I have learned to assess whether I can control it. Or not.

If I can, I take time to determine what action, reaction, or change of approach would serve me better, and I set out to do just that, calmly.

And if I can't control it, well I simply throw it in the f**k it bucket and let it go! Why let something I cannot control, control me?

This doesn't make me weaker than the person or situation at the heart of the challenging issue. It makes me stronger. So breathe, take a walk, journal, sit quietly and then make your decision based on how you genuinely feel.

This takes practise and it'll take time to achieve a level of equilibrium and control over your emotional responses. But I guarantee you will end up feeling so much stronger and proud to know you are now in control of your reactions.

When you achieve this, you can stop feeling like you are living life all wrong.

Challenges and change are inevitable, and you can choose stress, and react, or you can accept the challenge and respond. The first option is detrimental to your mental health, the second, an amazing way to take control of what happens to you, to stay true to who you are without compromising your health with drama, stress and anxiety.

If it isn't right, let it go

So many times, I have criticised myself, for not quite 'making the mark' or for needing to be better because I was not right for someone else. And I'm not just talking about romantic relationships, but relationships with friends, family, colleagues, even strangers.

We are so quick to allow other people's lives, stories and decisions reflect on us personally.

Truth is, the best friendships, the best relationships, the best encounters of any kind are never filled with drama or full of unsettled anxiety, they just are.

You know what I mean. When you think of your best friend, it just happened right? You love them unconditionally and never judge. You accept them as they are, and they do you.

People sometimes walk away. But it is not always all about you. The next time you sense someone is drifting away, talk to them, ask what is going on. You may be able to help them fix it or fix together. And if not, and they still choose to leave, be happy for them. It may still be painful but be content that they have chosen their way because it is right for them, not because you are wrong.

Don't fear forming attachments with others, just in case it doesn't work out and they leave. No-one is saying that when things do not work out, it doesn't suck.

But life is built on relationships of many kinds and to cut yourself off from them as a way of avoiding pain or loss, is not to live life whole.

Feeling of Togetherness is fine, good in fact. But never base your own self-worth on the validation of others. When it is not good for you, or for them, be brave enough to let it go.

"Life's truest happiness is found in the true friendships we make along the way"

Visualise your energy as a beautiful crystal

For a crystal to stay bright and beautiful, it needs to recharge, to soak in water, and bathe in sunlight or under a full moon.

When I visualise my energy as a beautiful crystal, it reminds me that my energy is precious, and it needs the chance to recharge to stay bright and strong.

If I am doing or feeling something that is draining my energy dry, dulling my glow or sapping my strength, I take a moment to consider whether it is worth the resource. If it is, I know I need to recharge and rejuvenate my own batteries. And if it is not, then I need to let it go.

There is a saying that you
can't drink from an empty cup or
pour with an empty teapot. So, decide, is
it worth doing what it takes to refill
the teapot?

As an example, you have a friend who is having a hard time, and you give all your spare time to lift them
up, help them, and reassure all will be ok.

But when you are done, you have no spare time left so your day has left you feeling a little flat yourself. Sometimes you are left with the monkey on your back and it is draining. But this is your friend, and you know they are worth your time, effort and energy.

So, make time to recharge your crystals. Soak in that bath, light those scented candles, bathe in the sunshine or relax in the moonlight, listen to that soft music, lose yourself in that book, drink that comforting herbal tea.

Never question yourself or feel guilty. What is good for you is good for all those around you.

Remember your oxygen mask goes on first, if you are going to be able to help others with theirs.

Loving YOURSELF is all-important

When you love something, you take good care of it. You do not neglect people or things that are important and precious to you. So why would it be ok to neglect yourself?

Show yourself some love, care, kindness and understanding. And do that for who you really are, not who you think other people think you should be.

What is this obsession we have all become slaves to, the need to look, be, act differently to gain validation from other people – even those we don't know, who don't know us and many who we will never meet?

Social Media. For all its benefits, social media has led to millions of people spending their time, money and attention on trying to live up to the picture of perfect created by filtered photographs and posts depicting supposedly perfect relationships and lives.

What it has done is create a widespread sense of failure, not being beautiful enough, successful enough, having the perfect home, family, children, holidays, cars, hobbies or skills. It has increased bullying, depression, jealousy, bitterness, bigotry and spite.

We are continuously led to believe that we don't have everything we need to be happy, to be healthy, to be a good mother, a good friend, the best employee, even that we don't look good enough for a picture these days, unless we filter this, filter that, make our eyes look bigger, our lips look luscious, eyelashes that reach to our hairline...

And, when we've done all that. We've bought into the edit apps, the 'magic' makeup, the spending on things we can't afford just to keep up appearances..... then what?

I confess to once having worked in sales, where you are 'taught' to find people's weaknesses and play on it, body shaming, being a common one.

I was not going to do that. If I was going to be in this business, I wanted to be real. I post information and stories of real women saying honestly what they feel about my business and what they got out of working with me.

Integrity is all, and I work best knowing that my intentions, support and motives are real and genuine. I take heart from the number of women who come to me, and stay, in their quest for self-improvement because they trust who I am and what I do. Actions and results speak louder than words and are far more valuable that the best of filtered photographs or fake life stories.

Letting go

It is never easy to trawl through things that once meant something special and accept that the time has come to let them go.

And I will confess, it took me a while and it took all my courage and resolve to get started. But once I committed to it, to physically and mindfully 'letting go', it was incredibly uplifting.

Anything thing, that no longer 'served me' or made me sad, melancholy or unwell, I ruthlessly, but mindfully, let it go.

The most painful was old photos of past relationships that I knew no longer made me feel good when I remembered, but nevertheless were a reminder of something that was once special.
But I was fed up with attaching past events to the present moment, triggering

feeling of inadequacy, sadness, failure or frustration, sending myself into spiral of 'remember when' or sadly wishing things were still the same.

I was not going to waste another minute of my present life looking back on things from the past that are not only irrelevant to my new life but bring me no joy.

So, I safely burned them. Off they went into the 'F**ck it Bucket'

And I felt all the better for doing it.

You won't eliminate your memories, the good ones or even those ones you'd wish to forget; but the truth is they don't have to influence your life anymore, they don't matter.... only today does.

This is My Story..... Yours is for You to tell

This is my story. It started out with as me just writing notes about how why I embarked on this journey to transformation. You will see some of it was planned, and some steps emerged as I progressed along the way.

But so many people have told me that they have been inspired by how I have changed my life, I thought that if my story can help other people, I'm happy to share it.

I have not set out to preach my journey as the right pathway for anyone, but if just one person can relate my experiences to their own life and use them to help achieve their own transformation to better things, it will be worthwhile.

I am not ashamed to say that I am happy with what I have achieved.

All I have achieved, all that I am now and all that I have in my life is a blessing, and in a huge way, I feel privileged, lucky and truly happy.

This has been a journey. I have not achieved this transformation overnight. It has taken time, persistence, patience and being kind to myself. And it has taken a lot of honest reflection.

It's not done.

I know I have more to do. But I also know I am well placed to keep going. No matter what I face, I am secure enough to know I can deal with it as it comes.

I just am! Here! Now and ok

Beyond thank you

I thank everyone who has helped get me here, including my family and, in particular, my wonderful son, you are my inspiration, my true supporter and the most compassionate soul I know.

To my friends, my truly great, honest, supportive friends who have always been there for me, I say thank you.

You all know who you are

Of course, not forgetting my two four legged babies Champ & Bella that love unconditionally and are charmingly fun company.

The time & love you have with all those who give time & love to you

is precious & priceless, live life with love, compassion and gratefulness, never losing sight of what makes life and the world better.

LOVE IN & LOVE OUT, PEACE, JOY, KINDNESS & CARE.

A WINDOW TO MY NEW WORLD.....

Excerpts from my Journal

I AM HERE NOW

I put my phone away, two days can I do it?

I am tired and disconnected.

I took the dogs to a local duck pond. It was falling subtle rain and circling the freshest air.

The swans greeted me first, and as usual my male
Frenchie dog, Champ, was curious, while my female Frenchie, Luna Bella, stayed

reserved and happy to
walk alongside me.

As I walked, with no contact to the
outside world, I was present.

I wondered did I feel sad, I couldn't
capture all this beauty through
the lens of my phone, I considered it and
then opened my eyes fully to the view.

I was here, now ....
We walked among the beautiful autumn

 coloured
dropped
leaves and
watched as
they
continued to
fall, I noticed
the leaves
move through
the wind and
fall into the
pond making
beautiful

shapes as they lay on the surface.

The raindrops fell and the circles moved
like they echoed through the ripples
merging into one like a family of circles
that belonged to each other.

A duck swam gracefully through them
and a straight line of ripples formed.

We continued to walk, and I noticed a
tree, solid and proud, it was central to
the view alongside the path we walked.
Something about it made me want to stop
and admire it.

I noticed the roots formed like a chair
that could hug you, so I took the offer
and placed myself down, leaning into
nature's hug.

A leaf fell gently directly onto my head,
which made me giggle and awaken my
thoughts...

I am here, now

Champ was getting a little too confident
and stepped into the water, gazing out to
the ducks and swans, until his head got a
little close to going under, I giggled again
as he ran back up to me on the path and
shook himself off. Luna Bella, still
curious but more cautious.

We continued our walk, and I took the
deepest breaths, I felt quite
emotional, yet so alive, and something
caught my eye. As I focused, a beautiful
heart hung alongside small, jewelled
decor & handmade gifts on the branches
of a tree.

The tree was a special memorial for
someone's mum, a grandchild's nanny,

I had previously picked up a beautiful
white feather on my walk, carrying it
with me, and I placed it among the gifts,
and a smile spreading across my face.

I decided to take a moment, looking out to the water on a nearby bench, I felt as though the words "thank you" blew through the wind, you have a good heart, trust and let go. I can't explain it, but I heard it loud, maybe it was my heart speaking it, maybe it was you.

I stepped toward the water directly in front of the bench, and there were a dozen or so ducks swimming slowly towards me, as if in a designated row, I had never realised how beautifully emerald green a duck's head was.

I felt the need to say out loud, I surrender, I let go. I cried, not in sadness, but with trust.

We slowly and mindfully headed back to our start point,

I loved how one circle path around a duck pond felt like so much more of a journey with a mindful eye and open heart.

A father, daughter and dog passed us by, with the father and daughter on their bikes, smiling and being together was enough.

It is hard not to appreciate simple beauty and life when you are awake.

Further into our walk back to the car, a vision of 22 pigeons sitting on a house rooftop across from the park, caught my eye. They were just perched, sitting as if they had scheduled to meet and enjoy the view together.

I looked across at the rugby field, and there sat dozens seagulls and one crow on the post and on the ground surrounding the area, it was a lovely sight to see, something I would have missed had I been walking with my phone in hand distracted. I even had the time to count them, all 34 of them, I had never seen so many birds all together.

Back at the car, the dogs jumped in and I realised, just looking at them,

how excited they had been to start our walk, and now, how content they seemed to have been outdoors having little adventures, simply taking it all in.

Where had I been?

I am here NOW

We got home and I gave them both a dog treat, warm bath and shampoo.

Then they placed themselves in front of the fire and cuddled up to sleep. As I write, to remember this beautiful mindful and awake meditation, they snore gently and in unison.

I did not need to capture it through a phone. I had it captured in my heart.

I am here, now ....

I AM HERE

As I sip on my decaf, I pull a face,

I forgot the sweeteners. My sweet
tooth still nudging me gently on
occasion.

I giggle and pop one in my warm mug of
pretend coffee, that has served me well.

I had energy, without crazy amounts of
coffee, it was a lovely reality wake up.

A lovely change I had made, and
something I appreciated for myself.

I looked at my two Frenchie dogs playing
with what looked to me like stupid dog
smiles on their faces. Happily, occupied
with each other

Needing nothing else.

I take another sip and look out the
window to see the sun, breaking up the
cold air, and warming up the raindrops
on my garden plants.

The orange and red leaves of autumn
filling the branches.

The tiny birds flying in and out of
my wooden birdhouse, enjoying the feed

And I Smile,

The time is now

I am here

Printed in Great Britain
by Amazon